Chronologic Calamity

B.A.M

Copyright © 2015 B.A.M
All rights reserved.
ISBN: 0692667962
ISBN-13: 978-0692667965

DEDICATION

I'd like to dedicate this first poetry book to all my support system; for believing that I had what it took to be the person I currently am today. You all keep me humble and passionate in life. Thank you and I love you.
-BAM

ABOUT ME:

My name is Brittanee but my friends call me BAM so you can call me BAM. BAM is short for my full name, also an exclamation of every result I do, and it also means night in Korean. I am a mixed baby. I have Filipino, Irish, American, Spanish, French, and Chinese in me. I have been writing since I was twelve years old. Ever since my 3rd grade teacher posted one of my poems on display I knew writing and becoming a poet is what I wanted to do for the rest of my life. I also have a big heart for helping people. I have created three advice columns on a site called Wattpad and have been doing that since 2013. My desire in life is to continue to help thousands of people in my lifetime through my writing and through the psychology fields. I believe that everyone needs someone to just give them a hand to hold and a friend to call their own. So I'd love to help you through your hard times and be a friend you will carry and remember through your life.

<3

Let's connect and get inspired together. Email me at: bam@bamcreativespace.com

CHRONOLOGIC CALAMITY

B.A.M

HOURLY REFLECTIONS

To reader: You can read my book from start to finish or you can pick a time in your day to read at an hour during the book and send me an email reflecting how you felt at the hour you read it. You can find my email in the about me section.

1	11 PM Frustration
2	7 AM Reflections
3	10 AM Thoughts
4	12 PM Heart Break
5	10:47 Tears
6	11 PM Genocide
7	10:33 Imagery
8	11 PM Naked
9	7 PM Turf
10	10 Minute Executions
11	10:48 Final Decision
12	8:13 Time Frame
13	9 to 10 Art Form
14	10:22 Acceptance
15	6 PM Blood Boil
16	6:40 Unstable
17	7:07 Feels
18	8:30 Awaken
19	22:08 Facts
20	22:30 Closure

CHRONOLOGIC CALAMITY

B.A.M

11 pm FRUSTRATION

I am your daughter
I am not enslaved with your decisions
Held captive in your traditions
Held down with your degraded intuition.
I do not owe you my blood and bones
Scrapped up by day to day loans
I am not a charity case
my piggy bank is not your safe "I need money" place.

I will not condone the bruises upon my leg
or the screwed up petty lies.
I will not believe the traded words of "Just one more Time."

I cannot be bought
or sold for a buck for your wallets pleasure.
I cannot be tied up
to your ways with lust and misfortunate adventures.
I shall not be manipulated.
I will not stand two feet underground.
I am not stupid.
I am not torn.

There is not a habit that can fix this mentality.
Chances mean as little as the nails cut off your fingers.
You do not own or rent this Temple.
You cannot please God with your ways of the devil.

I am encoded with your DNA.
But the password into my heart is more secure than the Empire State.
I am bestowed upon riches

CHRONOLOGIC CALAMITY

Even though I'm poor.
You are poor wishing riches would pour.

You try to hold me down
Letting me believe I am free.
But I am free because I stand greater than thee.
My willpower is strong
Stronger than my faith.
You cannot take away my life
Even if it was a mistake.

I am your daughter
Hear me clear
I am your daughter
But I am not you. -B.A.M

B.A.M

11PM Expressions
Free your mind with thoughts that hit at 11 at night here or write to express what you thought about the previous poem.

CHRONOLOGIC CALAMITY

B.A.M

7 AM REFLECTIONS

Jealousy
Coiled up into a ball thrown over the yard
Like garbage into a trash can
And that's all it is, its garbage.

To live with a green eyed monster is pointless
Because there are other people in this world
And I have to accept I am not your world,
Or at least not the only one in it

A woman once told me
"A woman knows to keep her mouth shut and everything is good at home."
And I wonder if that will be me 20 years down with the same mentality.
But I'm speechless
That woman is me, now.

I'm speechless because I stand by you whole heartedly.
And keep my mouth quiet on feelings I try to ignore.
Like its garbage,
Thrown over my shoulder by the table next to my bed
But I save it for later to read in the morning just one more time.

And it's threatening
Threatening to the mind, heart, body, and soul
But so addicting
I can't seem to get enough of its toxic fumes into my system
Love is the drug and you are the provider

CHRONOLOGIC CALAMITY

I'm addicted
Shoot a needle through my arm every day
For a taste of that feeling that makes my heart race
Injected with nauseous feelings
That I only get at seven am with you

B.A.M

It's 7 am. What's going through your mind? Write below.

CHRONOLOGIC CALAMITY

B.A.M

10 AM THOUGHTS

Veins pop out and breathing goes slow
I give all I have to the ones I know
I fight hard and strong
But there's always that sting
A sting of poison
A sting of love

A gentle hand
A hard hit
Skinny fingers sore
Big hands squeeze
Triumph and disaster
All mixed in one

No I'm not a sinner
Just a saint who a Devil's kissed

CHRONOLOGIC CALAMITY

You must have just woke up. Did you dream of anything? Write below.

B.A.M

Did you have your morning coffee yet? It's time to write. Express a time in your life where everything seemed to be chaotic and you wanted to stop the time. Let it be known where you would have rather wanted to be at that time.

CHRONOLOGIC CALAMITY

B.A.M

12 PM HEARTBREAK

Your words slip through the cracks of your lips
Leaving my heart to physically ache
Beat after beat
Slowing down each second as time passes

My mind wanders
As my eyes grow distant
Minute after minute
I am overshadowed by the blackness creeping in

Tears well up
To the threats that are called
I am not bothered
Just my worst fears coming to life

Another girl
Another promise
Another day apart

How do you bear the mistreatment?
The senseless under goat of betrayal
Broken promises

I have loved you day in and day out.
And it's scary,
Because I still will continue,

CHRONOLOGIC CALAMITY

Even with all the pieces of my heart spread onto your hands.

B.A.M

Do you remember your first heartbreak? Do you still think of it? Do you still feel it? Express it.

CHRONOLOGIC CALAMITY

B.A.M

10:47 TEARS

I love to say that I'm okay
But I know I could be wrong.

The tears fall down
Drop by Drop
Letting all my faith fall down

I don't know what is keeping me here
But I'll keep going in circles till I do

I try to trust the ones I love
But it's really hard to do

Embers spark
Just a glint
Not too much
Of hope

Maybe if there wasn't so much pain
I'll be able to hold your hand
Without letting go

I'm sorry if I push and shove
I just don't know how to stand
10 feet tall and super high
So nothing could touch me at all

Don't say it's just a phase
This has lasted years
Someone comes close
And I step away
Watching some disasters unfold

CHRONOLOGIC CALAMITY

I'd love it if I could feel
Safe in someone's arms
No question or doubt
Just the safest of sounds
Of knowing I am home

B.A.M

There's just days where the tears can't stop following and that's okay. Express why your tears are falling darling.

CHRONOLOGIC CALAMITY

B.A.M

11 pm GENOSIDE

What can I do…?
When I know what's right but hurts too much…
I'm burning into fire
Not escaping from any burns
Left into hot embers
Life sucked out and torn
I didn't want to be the one to cause this
But it's gotten to the point
Where the fire has covered me
No oxygen left to churn

CHRONOLOGIC CALAMITY

It's another restless night huh? Express it.

B.A.M

10:33 IMAGERY

A world within a cup
Casted trees
Flying birds
The moon along the rim
And the haunting of the smoke
Swirling among it all
It was poison but sweet
And she wanted to taste it all

CHRONOLOGIC CALAMITY

10:33 Keep your mind open. If you could live in a fantasy land. What would it look like?

B.A.M

11 PM NAKED

I am not crazy for the way that I feel
I feel the core of eternal pain
Coursing through each vein
Throbbing against my temples
Rushing to my heart
And attacking it with remorse
And my heart lies
It lies as it lies on the floor
Scourging out blood
So I bleed with trickles of retaliation
To every feeling that I have ever felt
When I was in love

And my love was deep
It was deeper than each cut I pushed a blade against my thigh
Deeper than each wound I carved into my arm
Deeper than each bruise I had made on my body
It was deeper than my soul could ever acknowledge
But my soul
Knows

It knows of each kiss I planted on each cheek
It knows of each touch I placed on your body
It knows of each time I spent spending time on you
And I now see my soul hurting just like my heart
But I am not crazy
For feeling the way that I feel

Because I felt at one point
I was the moon to your stars
I was the whiskey in your bottle
I was the God to your sands

CHRONOLOGIC CALAMITY

I was the sunshine on your gray days
I was the music on your sad ones
But I am no more

I am no more than the last girl
I am no more than the last heart wrenching conversation
I am no more than a girl being pushed to the side for another
I am no more than another story to tell that I have hurt you
And I have hurt you

I have hurt you with my insecurities
I have hurt you with my ways
I have hurt you with my actions
But I never tried to hurt you on purpose
So I moved
I moved on to try to give you better
And that may seem crazy but it's not

Love flies faster than a rocket into orbit
Runs faster than an athlete on their best day
Sours higher than a jet taking off in active duty
And stays
Stays deeper inside my flesh
Pushing its way past my blood stream
And into my heart
Where it explodes
But no, I am not crazy for how I feel
Because I will feel it again
Tomorrow

B.A.M

Express yourself. What was the most emotional time in your life and how did you get through it?

CHRONOLOGIC CALAMITY

7 PM TURF

Motion
The motion I feel stirring inside
Like a child running around in circles
Like a mother picking up her child
And the world flows with emotions
Sunk deep as we lay upon beds of grass
Feet sunk into water by sands
Tears dropped down into hands
I stare at the world with a hint of a smile
As the sun sets and the breeze becomes calm
A calm I can only feel when I am one with the Earth

B.A.M

The time is now 7pm. What's one thing from your day weighing on your mind? Express below.

CHRONOLOGIC CALAMITY

10 MINUTE EXECUTIONS

Cut off circulation
From body and mind
Pitter patter of my heart I try to ignore
The closeness of disappointment reaching its peak
Lost solidarity

B.A.M

If you only had 10 minutes left in this life to say the last things to your loved ones. What would you say? Express it.

CHRONOLOGIC CALAMITY

10:48 FINAL DECISION

I am cut off from all ties
I will not reproduce from your lines
I will stand down to who I try
My body is engraved with delicate times
I am my own belief
Even when I need God to keep me on my feet
You will not change me to your standards
I am independent and not standard
I will not let you play mind games
Games of a little boy with a mind cape
I am not troubled
Just abused
Bruised from the manipulation of dispute

B.A.M

10:48 It's time to share what's on your mind. Express it.

CHRONOLOGIC CALAMITY

8:13 TIME FRAME

Not at ease with my mind
Not at ease with the feelings I keep inside
Not at ease with the time
When it keeps turning and all I want it to do is rewind
When it keeps turning and all I want it to do is rewind
I'm not sorry for what I have done
But it is not easy to move along
Minute after minute
Step after step
I wish I could land on zero if it did ever exist

B.A.M

8:13 write a list of all the things you want to do in the next 8-13 years from now.

CHRONOLOGIC CALAMITY

9 TO 10 ART FORM

I am not the same
I will shed my broken skin again
Revive myself from any troubles
And the grace I have graciously appointed you with
will show in every art room
I will not be a tragisty
But a masterpiece of His creation
Fire blossoms behind my eyes
And it crackles inside my bones
It's the dictator of my soul
After 9 PM revelations
And before 10 AM revaluations
You will see my endless furry
In lines that will make your heart bleed
Finger tips hitting lips
While consciousness reminisce
I am not the same
My weaknesses are His

B.A.M

List 9 to 10 questions you would want to ask me or list 9 to 10 take-aways after reading the previous poem.

CHRONOLOGIC CALAMITY

10:22 ACCEPTANCE

Waste of space
Denial in our veins
Vain to our mistakes
Shutdown to each of our hearts
Knocked down into the black hole
As specks fly into orbit
Letting us reach but not too close
Closed out from the world
To rehabilitate our shape
We are but two planets
Creating an endless space

B.A.M

10:22 List the beautiful things in life that you appreciate.

CHRONOLOGIC CALAMITY

6 PM BLOOD BOIL

I will not stand for your petty lies.
I messed with you for a second and now you want to compromise.
I won't condone this hit one girl get another girl for free.
You're making babies like these women are a slot machine.
Don't tell me you don't comprehend your actions.
You know perfectly well they are a fraction.
You multiply legs like stanchions.
From bed sheets to your head games
I will not stand in front of you and guess change.
You are nothing to me.
Once was but now it's just how it was.

B.A.M

6PM We all get mad and that's okay. Express what makes you mad.

CHRONOLOGIC CALAMITY

6:40 UNSTABLE

I am built with building blocks
I hover over chimney tops
I tousle over colossal production
My motivation is my innovation
Surrounded by frustrated callings
One moment it's good another time I fall
But I build myself again and again
Until I finally stand stable

B.A.M

6:40
What makes you unstable?

CHRONOLOGIC CALAMITY

7:07 FEELS

Tell me why we have to get drunk to have a good time.
Use a gun to kill lives,
Abuse drugs to forget broken lines?
We use substance to power us when they only make us powerless when we are more than its power.

Even these days love destroys our hearts
And our hearts are the strongest muscle in our body besides our brain.

Our brain should work in millions of ways,
Instead of millions of ways we try and kill our brains.
I'm just saying…

Why are we sitting against blacktop?
Barely at the corner from the curb
Sticking our heads over bridges
Just a little too close to falling

Why are we using blades to weaken our skin?
When it should be used to sharpen and protect our will.

We are yet crumbling into weeds
And buying pot on the streets
And no, I'm not talking about a pot to hold a day's meal
But a plant to hold a stoners feel.
You see,
I'm just saying…

This world would do better

B.A.M

You just have to be a substance of a beautiful light
Instead of abusing substance that kills it.

CHRONOLOGIC CALAMITY

7:07
Your probably still in bed at the moment and that's okay. Sometimes I don't want to get out of bed either but instead of being all in your head alone. Express it below. Let me know what's on your mind too.

B.A.M

CHRONOLOGIC CALAMITY

8:30 AWAKEN

She lies in bed at night looking at the moon
Searching for answers against the stars
Quenched to be awaken

Hands pressed to her thighs
As fingers glide against her supple skin
And she bites her lips
Wishing he would bite her skin

And she imagines his lips pressed to her neck
Tongue swirling against her pulse
Hungry for the energy inside her

Heavy eyes fight to close
And they close
To dream about her Vampire

B.A.M

8:30
If you can dream it you can become it. Express your dreams below.

CHRONOLOGIC CALAMITY

22:08 FACTS

I am a vessel
I hold secrets and information that I could only obtain
from past episodes
It guides me as I prepare to come into war

My body is a Temple
It can only grow with growth from truth
Revealing a beautiful and liberating
Atmosphere as the day pursues .

I am yet a boundless princess
My tiara has fallen off so many times from worthless
occasions
But gets picked up and placed back into its position
from higher royals

I am bound to be a warrior
Because my armor was built inside my heart
So even if the enemy were to attack it
Love would attack back

And I am priceless
No price could price my soul
No penny can price my heart
No person can price my life

I am but a friend
A daughter
A child
Of God

B.A.M

22:08
Express the things you love about yourself.

CHRONOLOGIC CALAMITY

B.A.M

22:30 CLOSURE

I used to be in love
I used to be in a trance when I looked into your eyes,
Made its way to your lips,
Which couldn't stop starring into your heart, just like an x-ray.

I used to feel like our love couldn't die.
That it would have lasted longer than it had.
But I realized you didn't believe,
You didn't believe we would last more than we had.

And I was foolish to think that you felt my heart beating and breaking all at the same time.
To keep my breath from wavering or stopping from the things that was happening in our lives.
I was foolish to think you saw.

I was in love once.
I was in love with being in love with you.
With the thought that one day I'd be able to hold you and create a less hallow space
And crash with more beauty than our first hello.

But now as I look back to each day that brought me happiness
I can't ignore each day I was more in pain which love had to convince me to stay.

Staying was the easiest yet hardest thing I had to overcome with you.
Because I was in love
Yet love wasn't enough to hold you down.

CHRONOLOGIC CALAMITY

So I turned my back to my first love
Said goodbye to what we had
In each line that I write down
Erasing every memory of you
On paper

B.A.M

22:30
TIMES MAY SEEM A LITTLE HARD RIGHT NOW. IT'S NOT GOING TO STAY HERE FOREVER. EXPRESS YOUR FRUSTRATION, GREIF, HEARTACHE, AND EVERYTHING ELSE. EXPRESS IT BELOW. LET IT OUT.

CHRONOLOGIC CALAMITY

B.A.M

ACKNOWLEDGMENTS

I want to thank Mr. Tony for helping me construct and build my book as well as my creativity. To my Aunt and him for letting me express who I am. To my Parallel Diamonds family for motivating me and inspiring me in every aspect of my life. I also want to thank the ones in the past for contributing to my struggles, without them there wouldn't be anything to write about.

www.ingramcontent.com/pod-product-compliance
Lightning Source LLC
LaVergne TN
LVHW010026070426
835510LV00001B/4